The Seed Drill

The Seed Drill

Poems by

Ben Egerton

© 2023 Ben Egerton. All rights reserved.
This material may not be reproduced in any form, published,
reprinted, recorded, performed, broadcast,
rewritten or redistributed without
the explicit permission of Ben Egerton.
All such actions are strictly prohibited by law.

Cover design by Shay Culligan
Cover image by Becky Egerton
Author's photo by Robert Cross,
Victoria University of Wellington Image Services

ISBN: 978-1-63980-340-8

Kelsay Books
502 South 1040 East, A-119
American Fork, Utah 84003
Kelsaybooks.com

For my brother

Acknowledgements

My thanks to the editors of the following journals, where some of these poems—or versions of them—were first published: *The Clearing, Cordite, Ekstasis, Landfall, Magma, Otoliths, Relief, Signs, Solum Journal, Sweet Mammalian, Turbine | Kapohau, Whale Road Review,* and *The Windhover.* Thank you to the administrators and judges of the *VC International Poetry Prize,* the *Kathleen Grattan Award,* the *Christopher Smart/Joan Alice Award,* the *Beverly International Poetry Prize,* and the *Magma International Poetry Prize,* where poems from this collection have won recognition. Thank you to the administrators and benefactors of the Claude McCarthy Fellowship.

I'm grateful to Mikaela Nyman, Nikki-Lee Birdsey, Amy-Leigh Wicks, Max Chapnick, Anahera Gildea, Sarah Taggart, Cliff Fell, Damien Wilkins, Clare Moleta, Katie Hardwick-Smith, Jenny Bornholdt, John Dennison, Steven Toussaint, Robin Corney, Clay Nelson, Benjamin Myers, Michael Schmidt, Katie Manning, Mark Jarman, Jacob Stratman, David Mahan, Philip Armstrong, Kathryn Walls, Rochelle Thorn, Sofia Bue, Simon Littlewood, Sören Wulf (at Otto Wulf GmbH, the company who raised *Mary Rose*), and Karen Kelsay and Delisa Hargrove and the team at Kelsay Books, for their support, time, and care in so many different ways. A special thank you to Michael Symmons Roberts. This collection wouldn't be here without the guidance and encouragement of Chris Price and Peter Whiteford. And, Becky, thank you always.

Contents

I. Airworthy

i:	15
ii:	16
iii:	17
iv:	18
v:	19
vi:	20
vii:	21
viii:	22
ix:	23
x:	24
xi:	25
xii:	26
xiii:	28
xiv:	29
xv:	30
xvi:	31
xvii:	33
xviii:	34
xix:	35
xx:	36
xy:	37

II. Now and Not Yet

Now and Not Yet	41
Long Time Caller, First Time Listener	42
Calibration	45
Small Mercies	47
Skateboarders	48
Sand Caught by the Wind	50
Brass Rubbing	51
Cable Top	52

Last Supper	53
Love You Too	54
Star Wars in the Garden	55
Tenancy	56
Matins	57
Et Tu, Brute?	58
Dustsceawung	60
Abraham and Isaac	66
Notes on Five Bodies	67
I. Chalk Outline Detailing Position of Head with Knife in Hand, 1950	67
II. Victim's Feet Hanging off the Bed, 1934	68
III. Morgue, Man with Floral Tattoo, 1945	69
IV. Shoes, Arm, and Knife, 1950	70
V. Triptych of Images Tells a Story of Suicide, 1950	71
Relocation Specialists	72
Unknowing	73
Sola Gratia	75

III. /siːd/

:	79
Bad Seed	80
:	81
Ex Situ	82
Mingled Seed	83
:	84
:	85
:	86
Seed Money	87
Money Seed	88
:	89
:	90
:	91

Tilt | Shift	92
:	93
Cloud Seed	94
:	95
:	96
Magnetic Declination	97
:	98

Notes on the Poems

I.
Airworthy

i:

by laptop   by sweet by and by   by constrictive
    underwear   by un-pitter-and-un-patter of   by
    lack of   by the skin of   by rock-a-bye baby
      by 'transportation issues'   by a lifetime's
hot baths   by bye baby bunting   by hook and by
crook   by wreck of genetics   by all means
and none   not by might and not by power
but by night and *everydaylight* hour   by
love's labour   comes me   coming clean

ii:

is it wind   or tide   or recoil
    from discharging cannon broadsiding
    those pugnacious French   or
    pyroclastic cloud of anti-boarding
    net   or overloading   or poorly-
    distributed ballast   or ill-timed about
       or act of God   or 700
    accrued objects of George Carew's complaint
    I have the sort of knaves I cannot rule
    that is England's Vesuvius?

iii:

on the morning of the raising we rush
        to get a best view   50 five- and
        six-year-olds   scrubbed green and yellow
           no uniform hush of expectation   no hush
of cross-legged compliance   bolder
up on knees   damp with morning
rain and first breath   gardeners
at work already on beds outside
the steamed-up staffroom
        hang of smoke in this inner sanctum
        Mrs V__ (a few years hence her life cut short
by cancer) settles on the right station
        settles us for the live broadcast
from the Solent to bear witness
to overdue resurrection of the body
of Ol' King Harry's pride

iv:

because this body is a temple
        catacombs corridor its foundations
            chambers   crypts   vaulted ceilings
        —skeletal architecture of this underworld—
        stay sealed   empty   save for a waft of salt

v:

My doctor taps on his keyboard and peers at his screen for a few minutes. He prints a double-sided A4 factsheet, passes it across, briefly hanging limp between us. So much for general practising. Is it really so uncommon that he too must look it up online? I take the matter out of his hands. He returns to his screen while I read. He taps, peers again, and prints a label for the small sample pot he produces from his top drawer. *We will get,* he says, *to the issue at the bottom of this.*

vi:

lashed to a scaffold of yellow steel

    —emblazoned with its block-lettered promise
    BABCOCK POWER CONSTRUCTION
    DIVISION RENFREW TIPTON GRAVESEND

    held in tension at subliminal purgatory
Mary   cradled and cabled and free
of her   overburden hangs

halfway unsounded
              rock-a-bye
                          caved-in

    700 souls deadweighing her wrought frame—

Mary awaits late ascent

vii:

what vexes me (as I unslide the ranch
      slider of my rented holiday home
      and slip out to the dark deck) is the rash

      —nay, reckless—promise made by Abraham's
      God to Abraham   I have climbed the hills
      here and elsewhere and strained to hear him

      warn above the squall   but no voice calls
      to me from Kaukau or (today) Luxmore Peak
      no tongue cuts shrill through wind: no knife to kill

      the unoffered ram   no hereditary
      promise: no stars—this night nor any; only trapped
      warmth in the concrete under two bare feet

viii:

The sterile sample pot angled across my right hip like a sterile mouth mouthing a sterile welcome. I have history here. See how practised a move from Bible Hub to Pornhub my right hand makes (left taking it all in)—shower scene, MILF, American, *comely*; not-quite-muted volume—I'm almost enjoying myself, though it takes all my concentration to hold the pot in place with my right wrist whilst beating rhythm with my left and holding the laptop steady—that childish trick of rubbing your belly and patting your head at the same time.

She steps from the shower and shows herself to me. *The fair breeze blew, the white foam flew, the furrow followed free.* With relief I close this one-shot deal.

(Please, keep a lid on it.)

ix:

past George Carew lying askew under his silty sheets;

past his then minute Royal Highness
       peering from ramparts of history
       all speck of fur and hat and rage and too
       far ago and too long away for TV to make out
       his words or read his protesting lips;

past his now Royal Highness this Prince
       of Wales dressed for TV in naval garb
       and Burberry trench, cap-on-head lip-read
       and close-up in the overseer's launch;

past the landmarking lens of the BBC;
       fleeing French; living rooms; classrooms,
       staffrooms, stuff of a drizzly Monday;

past *rock-a-bye Mary on Tog Mor's tops | for the wind*
       blows, the cradle it rocks | now the steel breaks,
       the cradle does fall | down nearly comes Mary
       and cradle and all;

past cannon-salute (two six-year-olds die
       in a staffroom finger-gun shootout);
       past champagne and smoke-boom;

       she surfaces in the twentieth century

x:

the road is not reliable this time
       of day   but doctor's orders are simple:
       sample   still at body temperature
         to the JR within the hour

not so ancient as to have conveyed
       conscripts and oak to the shipyards   not so
       modern to have been spared burdens of war—
       Empress, Isis escapologist, snow-
       white Maude   Welford   Greenham women
         Roundhead   Cavalier tread visible from its
       passing windows—

north: Oxford   south: Winchester   Southampton
       Southsea Castle   between: the A34
       the way the kingdom divides

xi:

two brothers turn-take to raid and patrol
       the Kennet and Avon canal   stealth up

       its wooded flank unnoticed
       from the service road below and leap out

       onto the towpath   cock and raise an invisible
       rifle and pull its trigger   swap

       such undercover action repeats
       from the sewage works until halfway

       to the tithe barn
       where one soldier is abruptly snared

       in no-man's-land
       by a camouflaged curl of rusted barbs

       an iron warp with bramble weft draws
       the campaign's first blood

they grow with me   two thigh-length scars
       parallel front lines of a childhood war

xii:

    he attempts metaphor   *Imagine*

> *you're firing arrows. There aren't many*
> *arrows in your quiver. And their fletching's*
> *in poor condition. Besides, for those arrows you*
> *do have, there's insufficient draw on your bow,*
> *your yew doesn't provide enough power.*

    blank look

    my doctor doesn't make any sense   or
    I can't understand my doctor   or my
    doctor doesn't understand what he's
    talking about   or   at the very least
        my doctor doesn't know how to make
    what he understands understandable

    blank look   he attempts simile

Your sperm is like a fleet of ships. Her egg
    is like the enemy's defences, and it's
    like your fleet hasn't got enough ships
    in it. And most of them flounder
    after leaving harbour. And
    of the few that engage, well, they don't have
    the energy to broadside.
    There is, if you like, no firepower.

blank look   (and no I wouldn't like)

       the technical medical diagnosis—
       motility, morphology—he knows
       I won't understand
                   sorry   I need
       bluntness from him   *your semen*
       is too weak   *you don't produce*
       enough seed   *God's given you a purse*
       of debased currency   *there's fuck all*
       we can do   I want *conviction*
       from him   that *children are a heritage*
       the fruit of the womb a reward

unexpected directness   like the time
       Mr C__ told us all in PE to show some spunk
       and we froze   then sniggered
         and he got angry and kept us in
       at playtime and   when he went off
       for tea and a cigarette   Marcus H__ kept us
       entertained with dirty jokes   like a salty
       seadog setting recruits at ease

xiii:

we rank-and-file to our classroom   press
    dead-headed matchsticks and lollypop sticks
    into service as forty acres of oak
    and a thick strip of keel elm

    run ribbon and paper up our pencil
    masts

        as if somehow expecting
an unwrite of history
we unruly Henrys and Helens hail
our fifty Marys   our faithful reproductions
    our waterloose craft   on the tadpole pond

    and watch knaves scupper the lot

Mrs V__ wades in with her pond-dipping net

    one craft   no one knows whose   dangles
    dry from a branch

xiv:

a civil war clash; a familial
        dispute   two brothers defend / attack
        the motte of sand at the builders' merchant

        S__ shins up the siege machinery
of the bay's block wall   crowns
himself as castle king   he rains
down hardened clumps of sand sometimes
bright and sometimes dark

I dig in as
        sand grenades   sand Greek fire   sand cannonball
          sand mortars   sand cluster bombs
        all manner of sand incendiary devices and sand-
        held IEDs   target my position   my head   hair
          eyes   down the back of my t-shirt   inside
        my shoes   socks   shorts   *appearing either*
more or less impregnated with earth and cinder

I lie defeated
                a contorted Pompeiian   in rehearsal

XV:

modern medicine applies its own ritual: a—ppearance, p—ulse, g—rimace, a—ctivity, r—espiration. Craned clear of the water, *Mary* needs water. Neither airworthy, nor waterworthy, she's apnoeic; she'll not fight nor fly, even in her pre-breached state ill-equipped to navigate these currents. Thoroughly exposed to this other she glistens in the ether—slumped to one side, breathless—drying in her cradle, dying despite the drizzle. All joy falls to lullaby, falls to rite; falls to Margaret's rule: lift, catalogue, conserve, tag, bag.

The admiral leaves a wife, leaves no children.

Lifting leaves the bed depressed.

xvi:

    as every prog-rock fan and historian
        knows, Jethro Tull invented
        the seed drill   though technically
        refiner or *perfecter,* and *author* on
        husbandry, rather than inventor

        as there's evidence of Chinese,
        Babylonian, and Mughal drilling,
        both before and after the Seed of David
        grew to bloom: human
        inheritance predicated
        on faithless reproduction,
        insemination through artifice
        at the very heart of us   a chorus
        of all comers, all corners

                      despite
        his diagnosis not yet sinking in,
        or perhaps *because* his diagnosis hasn't
        yet fully sunk in, my doctor changes
        tack to outline the choices

            one involves extracting more sperm
        (MILF, again), adding hormones—heaving it
        from a warm bed at dawn and out
        for inspection—then returned fit to serve

            time and again I've done the seed drill
            this time it's the seed for-real

We have, he says, *a number of things*
    we could consider, as if he too
    is struggling with his own line
    of succession, *before*—a micro-pause

like the *um* after a joke—*we think*
about in vitro, or non-medical options
such as adoption and the like . . .

. . . the like? (again!)   like prayer?
theft? adultery? a break with Rome?
    forensic archaeology
of my own backstory to unearth
how I've hastened my own
end?   (besides, I've already tried
a couple   no luck)   or dig
further back on my father's side
to expose some small sin
that sits on the statute books
somewhere between murder
and a minor misdemeanour
like drunk in charge of a horse—punishable
neither by fine
nor hanging but by slow strangulation
of the male line

xvii:

What now? Low sky, done deal, irreversible position, that fullness of rain after rain. Names picked out must be put away, plans need shelving, conversations to avoid: such is the untaking of things. *Your decision, after all, is binding,* the doctor'd said. The way we only notice what we don't want to notice: brow furrows of every passing driver, frothy whites of each eye; their silent inside singalongs; Velcro rip of traffic through standing water.

xviii:

part museum part mausoleum   a public exhibition
        brittle as walnut shell   open
            raw   empty as his half-promises

xix:

IC BEN GHEGOTEN INT IAER MCCCCCX
       barber-surgeon's preserved right index fingerprint
            in a sample pot of fossilised ointment
       thimble ring
       mortar of peppercorns
       one bone angel
       102 tonnes of makeweight (flint, cockle-,
            periwinkle-, oyster-shell)
       nit combs
       bones of rat   frog   mongrel
       fleshless seamen
       purse of debased currency

these—and more—the salvaged hulk bestows

XX:

    a Pompeiian household head propped up on elbows takes
        one lasting look at his unhusked family   one

        wrapped in swaddling clothes lies
        in her consumed crib   one rages

        against fallen-in sky   one assumes her recovery
        position at the foot of the stairs   one hunches

        as in a corner with a finger to an arid
        eye   one—*what the hell*—is (claims an online

        tabloid) enjoying a final fiddle, hard
        at work on his eternal erection

        while the bay burns   two fold onto each other
        in an out-of-register yin/yang   one in agony

        is caught mid-writhe   and another   and
        another   and one prone

        to prayer clasps hands below her chin   one
        asleep tucked under his long-shrugged covers

and a dog   and a horse   against the gallery black
        they are astronauts untethered in utter space

        or synchronised swimmers who've fallen
        out of all time   cast   *in absentia*

            as innocents in this dumb show   as rocks
        which might at any moment sing

xy:

not by might and not by power   but by night
       and *everydaylight* hour   by love's labour
           comes me   comes me   coming clean

II.

Now and Not Yet

Now and Not Yet

S__ and I race upstairs to the bedroom
that overlooks the river and railway
and away to the White Horse and cement-
works chimney whose plume
rises like a speech bubble to become one
with this articulation this deep grey-
white cloud-accumulation of plosives
and uvulars where all air folds and rolls
and we hold our breaths because when we breathe
we fog the panes centimetres
from our noses as we scan for that split
second of cracked white heat at the centre
of everything, which we can't feel
but something somewhere does, and
when we do see one never directly always
on the periphery we play our new-learned
game of slow counting the silence until
the *son* catches up with its *lumière*
to hear how near to us thought's light makes landfall
one Mississippi two Mississippi
three Mississippi . . . eight Mississippi
nine Mississippi every five rivers
is a mile from here and we imagine
near Westwood a reverse socket of singed earth
the current's flowed into or startled
Friesians in fields halfway to Staverton
where one unlucky cow
didn't hear it coming until after she saw it
by which time it was too late
and despite us not knowing to misquote Heraclitus
lightning never step-leads into the same
place twice we scour our propagated
sector of sky and go on counting
on the light to keep announcing itself.

Long Time Caller, First Time Listener

It's late, gone nine. I'm driving home
from Palmerston North along the back road

through Tokomaru and Shannon after
another session with the teachers. There's

never consistent reception on this road.
It's not until you're almost at Levin

that you can hear what Bryan is saying
on *Nights* on RNZ. So I auto-seek

because it's not good to drive this stretch alone
with your thoughts, especially after

a session with the teachers, especially
as parts of this road are so dark. The worst

patch is around Tokomaru. The steam
museum at Tokomaru still hasn't sold.

About 18 months previously I didn't take
this back way to and from Palmerston North

with my parents because I didn't want dad
to see that it was for sale and think

it would be a good idea to buy it.
There's a good reason why steam museums

on back roads to Palmerston North remain
on the market for so long. The auto-seek

settles on a talkback station. The host
provokes his callers with his devil-

may-care attitude and his devil's-
advocating and it's easy to be an advocate

for the devil when you're broadcasting
to people driving in the dark

heading home on back roads to Wellington
when the reception is a bit iffy.

You might even expect to see the devil
loitering at the crossroads, like with Robert

Johnson down on his knees in Mississippi, except
in the Manawatū at the junction

where State Highway 56 meets State Highway 57—
which would have taken the blues

down a different route. The topic
isn't all that controversial, something about dairy

export prices. This year farmers aren't getting
their forecast dividend. The fields I drive past

are full of cows whose production worth
might be less than it was on my way up.

The Manawatū is still dairy country
by night. But there are methane flares

that may or may not be aliens—
or aliens that may or may not

be methane flares. The methane flares
probably interfere with radio

reception, especially if they're real
aliens. Perhaps living with the threat

of aliens is another reason
why steam museums linger on the market:

steam can't really compete with alien technology
any more than cows can. About 3km

from Levin, still on the back road, more or less
where the streetlights start, I flick back

to *Nights with Bryan Crump,* cutting off
the talkback host just as he's devil's-

advocating for dairy nationalisation.
And in the re-tune there is the briefest

of pauses like in the surprising emptiness
of a lighter-than-expected box or that breath

after a gust of wind has just blown through—
and you're standing at the mouth of the wind's cave

in the silence of high mountains and the silence
of heaven—when for the first time

on the back road I really listen and the reception
is so *crystal* my ears tingle.

Calibration

Who can ascend
these hills, O Lord?

And how quickly? Who
has a stubborn heart

and sure feet
and a strong GPS signal?

I look at Dai: *Ready?*
That sounds like something

I might have written,
he replies. I should've known

he doesn't use
a fancy watch. And he's got

those sandals
like the Tarahumara wear,

those barefoot running ones
all the rage a while back.

After all his run-less years
Dai's calves

still hold their definition
but his middle

has spread a bit—
a middle that never once

bore the weight
of another

king's armour; calves
to deliver him

from lion, bear, giant;
the balls

to invite
another man's wife

to his bed—so we have
one thing in common

at least. *Don't you miss
being outside?* I ask.

*That's why I write about
it all the time,* he says.

Small Mercies

Never you. Always a friend of a friend of a friend
who knows someone who missed *that* flight, who drove
the taxi which picked up ghost passengers, whose
recovery defied medical science.

Is it enough for you to be home
when the courier calls, to miss the car
you didn't see when reversing from your parking space,
to know that—in the end—it was quick

and there was no pain? Miracles are only
ever third- or fourth-hand, a hand-me-down
laying-on of hands, something divined
rationalised, *explained*. And you don't see

the signs because there are none: presence
you read as absence, absence you read as gone.

Skateboarders

skateboarders on the hill again   after
midnight   after quiet   their little round

wheels tear down the bends on the traffic-
free hill   whoop round the hill's rubber-wheeled

bends   woken   their little hands on little
outstretched arms keep the invisible walls

from closing in   their round rubber whoops ring
down the hill   ring them round the swan-necked bends

    full awake   after light   after quiet
    skateboarders tear in doppler shifts   swan down

the hill moon-lit   stereoscope through the swoop-
necked bends   balance outstretched arms   bend-

push a moon-lit whoop round the neck   their
little hands follow the swan in little

clenches   after midnight hands tear me up
    widen me awake   skateboarders doppler

clench with their after-light hands outstretched to
the neck of the swan   their little traffic-

free hands tear at the bends   moon-lit swan
is awake   its little legs and little feet

tear at the bends   can't stop   outstretched arms
and little rubber hands form their clenching

    little round stereoscopic swan whoops
doppler swoop at my after quiet   on-

the-hill-again skateboard hands ring the swoop-
neck of the swan   whoop for joy when it's done

Sand Caught by the Wind

to think of atoms: might be
brownian motion here   random
as love or lovers in bumper cars
lurched this way then that   but
is *sour-sweet*   directionless
    tossed on a strong northerly like
drawn paisley wisps on seaside tarmac
    a dancing calling card   it
is as light shafting through cornered dust

Brass Rubbing

S__ and I step from summer-holiday
sun into cool twilight of church,
its fusty silence broken
by the clack of our sandals on flagstone
as we down-aisle to the apse
where, under the glass-eyed gaze
of confectionery-wrapper apostles,
we find a good one. With our sleeves
we brush dust off the monumental
brass of the knight *hic iacet corpus*
and *hic etiam iacet* his good lady.
Mum hands us sheets
of butcher's paper and we hunch
on hassocks over them
as if at prayer, heelball and bronze
crayons in our hands.
For an hour nothing
but the furious trundle of wax
on paper on latten on limestone
on our knees, each pass
darkens the heraldry of the dead.

Cable Top

she asks me about lying   what I think
of lying   is lying ever the right thing
to do   those aren't her exact words   I can't recall
her exact words because the lying part
of me is on the defensive   while she asks
I watch a bird caught
in the cable car terminus   —a sparrow
possibly something larger   I've always wished
I knew bird names—   hardwired for sunlight
it darts at the uppermost north-facing windows
& I hate & love
the architect for designing this attractive trap   all air
& polish   despite the cruelty
I've always had a soft spot for birds
in buildings   feather ghosts
in the concrete machine
& I think this is a metaphor   —the bird is me
programmed to slam against the glass
as I seek light   ignorant of an easy out
of whatever elegant system
I'm caught in—   consider she says
if true is only true with its counterweight
lie   if true is only true
when you understand the lie   until then
it's a bird at the glass   greedy for light
as a firstborn for his inheritance

Last Supper

Don't worry, *my little sparrow,* about what to eat
tomorrow or the day after that or the day
after that, or what to drink. There are puddles, pools
on the roof, reservoirs in gutters and gardens
for you to sip and splash in. You'll find scraps under
the tables and benches (watch out for dogs!).
My little sparrow, you can't follow me. Your wings
won't carry you. But I'll be back. Not like this, not
here, not sure when. You'll find me one spring morning
in the ornamental gardens, by the bandstand
and pond, doling out breadcrumbs like seed. I'll wear
a coat and hat (iridescent feather in the band
so you'll *know* me). I'll be feeding the koi, leaning out
beyond the fence so the smaller ones get their share.

Love You Too

The waxing moon picks out
a sinuous declaration of love
sprayed on the railway bridge
at Crofton Downs. In the sweep
of headlights, in the briefest
of under-passings, few might think
the graffitied panels worth a look,
much less of the one who signalled his heart
between rivets, on rust, in white—
or notice how that white slow-corrodes
into permanent scar. For even
after over-painting or chemical
scouring, ferrous skin remembers.
Imagine him up there, finding something
in the thin air to hang on to.

Star Wars in the Garden

beyond the window and into green-
as-envy bush bleeps a *tūī*
    chuckle   whistle   stoppal
    issuing robotic shrill like
R2D2   I'm expecting
a display   holographic image
    a beaming on the leaves with those
isoscelean lines that come to
rest on a blue beckoning princess

Tenancy

Offered his pick of the rooms he takes the attic.
Pulls up the ladder, disappears into pitch,
beds down between boxes, crockery, clothes. Fashions
someone's old garish coat for a pillow—unsightly stain
folded inward. Removes tiles to drink
from the guttering, coaxes blackbirds (he has time
on his side) to bring crusts, fruit, early-season berries.
It's not long before they forget he's up there—creaks
blamed on poor pipework, thumps explained as *weather*
or ghosts—so they move on. Others move in. Install
double glazing, fix the plumbing, mend the roof. Yet still
they stir in the night, unsure what the small noise is.

Matins

she leaves me
Ilya Kaminsky
on a WhatsApp voice memo
I have come, God, I have come
running to you
her voice clean   clear
as bones
picked of flesh
& warming in this lengthening
morning light   her recount
a figment of someone
else's imagination

Et Tu, Brute?

> Hamlet: A man may fish with the worm that hath eat of a king, and eat of the fish that hath fed of that worm.
> King: What dost thou mean by this?
> Hamlet: Nothing but to show you how a king may go a progress through the guts of a beggar.
> —Shakespeare, *Hamlet,* Act IV, Scene III

Heading up Paekākāriki Hill Road,
apropos of nothing, I mention
that although I don't believe in karma
or reincarnation, I do believe
in reincarnation *of a sort*. For instance,
when they transplant another's heart
into another's chest, there's evidence
of cellular memory: donor's
traits—fluency in foreign tongues,
quick temper—donated too. In the dead
of night months later the new-hearted cold-sweats
a stranger's dream, days damned by déjà-vu,
a vegetarian craves pork.

Every bit of us is second hand.
Is it too far a stretch to believe
molecules from rat shit, an extinct bat,
matter from the heart of distant star,
a flightless bird from our neck
of the woods, are me or you—*us*? We take
a bend a shade too fast, I reach for the handle
above the door trim. They say that when knifed
in the back Caesar breathed out his last
litre of air and that—two thousand years
on—each of our breaths contains one molecule
of his. Does that go for anyone
who died two thousand years ago?

At the summit the road swings right
and down to the left Kāpiti Island and the sea.
The part I can't get my head around
is how primitive it all is: between chests
they pack the heart in ice in a chilly bin.

Dustsceawung

:

After her mother dies she thinks it good to dig her plot:
nineteen metres by thirteen, and given
over to goosegrass and offcuts of carpet, tucked

in the far corner of the allotments. Handing her
a rabbit trap and keys, one for the height-
restricted access gate one for the well lid,

the Association Chair warns: *Sure you know
what you're in for? It's not something
to be undertaken lightly.* It's dark for May

that stormy dark before clouds break, before rain pelts
and veins as blood in rivulets and streams, and scabs
as puddles, before it skins stalks, leaves, fruit, road, town.

A procession of early starts and warm mornings: she
scythes the weeds, unpeels sticky carpet-plasters
to expose, each time, fresh dirt sores. And each time

bugs of polished black skitter into the lace tangle
of grassroot. Worms bore for cover. For borders she lays
long lengths of scaffold plank, runs a rotavator

through the matted soil, takes with good grace handouts
from Alberto, her neighbour (*You know, while you wait
for yours to grow*), and swaddles the grazed wound

of earth with palls of thick plastic sheet. She sets to work.
In her new feint-lined notebook, a plan: carrots, beans, cabbage,
currants; sketched orange, green, blue, black.

:

Bonfire, from *bone fire, bone fyre, bane fyre,
bane fire*: fire in which femur, scapula,
skull, ribcage, spine (frequently still an integral

part of the martyr, heretic, criminal, book)
and other flammable, disposal items burn.
Regulations state wind must not blow from the west

so as to prevent a smoke hazard for drivers
on the adjacent dual carriageway when bonfires
are lit. After weeks of unseasonably late spring sun

her pile of skeletal grass is ready to light.
She wonders whether a square of carpet will burn.
Decides not. Instead she flaps it to fan the flames.

Alberto's allotment is Arcimboldo's oil painting
Reversible Head with Basket of Fruit:
beet, carrot, courgette, plum, radish, all organic

in shade, shape and imitation of body part.
His soil is immaculately tilled: no weed,
stone or footprint. He protects paradise with roof

and walls of half-inch gauze, tacked to a pergola
that runs length and width. More delicate fruits of his
labour stew under greenhouse glass. At the overlap,

where net-ends meet, no white-clad angels stand guard
with swords aflame—just a thick, raised, ring of potash
and small blue pellets to keep snails and slugs at bay.

Collusion of head and heart. A rabbit—grey scrag ears
taut like beech leaf, like mussel shell, furious pulse
barely visible—presses himself so far back

against the cage end that he square-inches his fur
on the wire. Two almond eyes follow her. Once he scents
her half-chance of indecision—too squeamish to put him out

of his misery, too sensible to let him loose—
he's up, paws on the door, thumps in sudden palpitation.

Now zoom out.

Go high.

Look down
          on each small plot with its own trapped rabbit. Higher
yet, arrhythmia as far as the eye can see. She mutters an oath
under her breath, sets this heart free. *Go on, beat it.*

:

A word for the contemplation of ruin, decay, dust
and its associated melancholy: 'dustsceawung.' Common
or garden dust? Before us, before her, before all of this

horses free-rein'd here on Abingdon Common.
The main road west through Marcham little more
than a bridle path, a packhorse track rutting up the hill

past the Crown to Frilford and out to the Bath-Oxford
coach road. South, flat country to the Ridgeway,
floodplain bordered north and east by river and town.

Open loamy land, unshadowed, and sown with teasel
and hoofprint is, for her, parcelled off—
her portion and her cup, her considering of the dust.

Now with her whole lot secure she takes her blinkers off.

Abraham and Isaac

I am up well before night leaves the hut
to draw water and light our Primus stove
to make tea before waking the boy. Let
him sleep in a little, I think. Breakfast
done we put on camouflage and prepare
the rifles. I tidy up, give the boy
forty-five minutes' head start but I catch
him in a patch of bush three clicks downstream.
Crouched there, he looks just like a white-tailed deer;
how still he twitches and sniffs the air to pick
a scent that I imagine antlers either side
of his close-cropped head. I raise my rifle.
With the deer in my sights, I wait for a voice
to tell me when to squeeze the trigger.

Notes on Five Bodies

I. Chalk Outline Detailing Position of Head with Knife in Hand, 1950

Watch: chalk summons
its template
conjures its core

from sleeping dust
pulls—*from where?*—wind
that disperses finer grains

cleanses lungs, restores
each corner with pulsing breeze
like flinging windows open

on a clear spring day.
He spits out blood
as skin and bone re-fuses

he stands, dresses, folds
the blade back
into its handle, slips it

into his jacket pocket
runs his bruised right hand
through his regrown hair

goes to find a bus.

II. Victim's Feet Hanging off the Bed, 1934

head where his soles should be
shoes pavement-side up and hooked

over the end of her bed
    scuffed   undone   mouth agape

    throat exposed   a cavity
from where no sound will come

but complaint and twist and creak
of skin   loose tongue

    looser as laces plucked
between finger and thumb relax

the fit   there's something   still
    in its stiffness   new

leather expects and resists its foot
    his spectators

new that morning (receipts confirm)
yet to submit to discipline

of horsehair and Shinola   quick spit
and he's given a good once-over

    polishing off
a job for the night before

III. Morgue, Man with Floral Tattoo, 1945

All things pass, he said:
                          pain from the carnation
needled onto his upper arm
                          irrational

fear of permanence as the first seeds
are sewn and sown
                          bruise budding across skin

worry that keeps him awake at night
                                guilt
hanging like pre-dawn mist.
                       Everything

slows and loudens when light goes
                            amplified
in its chamber of nocturnal echo.

And how right he was:
                       now, three days cut,
the bloom already gone
                       petals

one by one
            quietly flicked
to the ground
                  soon the stem will give.

IV. Shoes, Arm, and Knife, 1950

Flung impotent across the apartment carpet, the victim's arm points to something of the Sistine ceiling. Michelangelo placed Adam naked and louche in Eden, used God's outstretched right arm to lay a finger in blame. Here the arm is as lifeless as those Oxfords paired next to it. And the knife, more letter-opener than stiletto, *planted*—the prosecution alleges—on the open palm *to make it look like suicide*. Blade barely three inches long, hilt intricately carved, curled pommel to prevent sliding in use. Ornate, yes, but perfect to slip into a belt or tuck between a deity's ribs.

V. Triptych of Images Tells a Story of Suicide, 1950

1. Car parked in garage

Sooner or later someone should reverse
the car back out. Upholstery requires
scrubbing and the splatter above the door
needs a dab of peroxide, then saltwater.

2. Body on back seat of car

Up in the eaves, spiders have spun silk,
too much of it. A waste. Holes blown
through it catch only stale air
and shadows. Nothing sacred here.

3. Detective

Framed in the rear window, the officer
stands hands on hips, head cocked to one side,
cap and sunglasses on. Warm enough
to unbutton his jacket but not to take it off.

Additional details

Notes of orange blossom, jasmine,
and scent of dust in late-spring heat.

Relocation Specialists

Following a policy change all flora
and fauna seized at our borders are no longer
incinerated. So now bio-officers in crisp shirts

and surgical gloves catalogue today's seized
specimens—Star of Bethlehem, sycamore key,
mustard seed, common adder—and place

them in plastic crates. Later when tubs, tanks,
cages fill relocation specialists cart the haul
thousands of miles to an uncharted island south of here

where scientists re-wild. Measures
are taken: existence denied, entries expunged
from all records, names quietly forgotten.

Unknowing

you can't see the summit
from the carpark for cloud

but when you reach it
you're accepted

into the weather   as into
a place a child might choose

    somewhere to see from
but not be seen in

    & you take it all in—
the white car

on Wilton Road
    its headlights reflecting

in the wet tarmac
    pitch markings

on the park   flank
of suburb laid out opposite

like a butcher's chart—
    you run yourself

to the edge
of exhaustion on your assault

on the hill   six times
since last December

via this route   up & back
& what for?   your father

once asked, *what are you
running from?*   he never asks,

*who are you
running towards?* you don't seek

or expect anything
except to catch something

of his silence   to run
downhill through the pines

Sola Gratia

As he gets up from the table,
catching the waiter's eye

and gesturing with his hand,
he says, *my friend will pay.*

III.

/siːd/

:

that seeds wind-blown or beak-spilled find fissures
that sun-fed and mist-swaddled they cleave solid rock
      that granite yields to green
that permanent cedes to the creeping roots of these
      juvenile upstarts and birds
                          lodge in the branches and sing

     sing

              sing

       such songs

Bad Seed

Take this bird: see how it jumps from branch to branch,
how it stitches its feathered self behind leaves as you
walk in the garden in the cool of the evening; how you
hear its shy trill as shame, naked notes shivering
in falling light.

```
            soil                              soil
               seed                              cede
    rain                              rein
                  dew                                  dues
            sun                              Son
    root                              root out
                  field                                yield
            fill                              fall
               stem                              stem
                     bough                              bow
       incipient                        insipient
*adamah*                          *Adam*
                  bloom                                blood
            scent                              ascend
```

Ex Situ

He made you a little lower than the angels, the same
angels who now cower—as if pinned
against the wall—behind the door to your room, who
make themselves impossibly slight for when the door
swings back, who quire themselves thin and enfold
their light two, four, eight sheets deep in the crook
of the hinged door's elbow, as you swear blind
they'll never darken your doors again, nor you theirs.

Mingled Seed

Alongside the hedge, white-on-green seed company
signs—*Plenitude, Abundant, Approved, Resilience,
Fertile, Bounteous*—slogan'd in fonts designed to be seen
at speed read like a roadside roll call of Puritans' wives.
Around this field, host to its crop trial, you tread
as she takes black-and-white pictures of apple boxes
inside the rundown cottage at its heart.

Your visitors are here. They speak to you
in your language and tell you what you already know
of your homes, your gods. They wear your clothes.
They talk you into bed and you let them
sleep with you, seduced by familiar words on unfamiliar
tongues. Up and awake before the visitors, in the dewy
silence of the morning, you try their words for size,
like a new convert quoting from the minor prophets.

Between the *goodly* and *upright* stalks, scraps of black ploughed plastic flap like wings of interred ravens—all punished, so the story goes, for one mating on the ark, spilling his seed into her beak.

:

The half-life of faith: Archimedes asked for a long lever,
a fulcrum and a place to place it. But his demand
is for something no bigger than a mustard seed: packaged
as Semtex, replacing ball bearings in bullets, as tongues
of fire on tribal weddings, substitute for plutonium
to obliterate the gates of paradise. All along
the mountains are not so much as climbed.

Seed Money

Less angel investor, more someone who smells potential:
she has a good nose for things on a good head
for business. It's understood she's looking
for a significant return on her investment. You incubate
in polytunnels, measured in football pitches, plastic
visible from space. You catalogue and fertilise your seed
in optimum conditions. Halogen lamps stimulate round-
the-clock photosynthesis. And patrolling the aisles—for
aphids, signs of growth—are white-coated gardeners,
forever cursed to tread between ever and amen.

Money Seed

To reverse engineer an offering   to deconstruct
these minted promises—most of which have circulated
for years without ever making good—   to unfold trust
like you butterfly a chicken   to un-sum parts
into pieces worth less than themselves   to reduce
operating capital to tithes and widows' mites
    to identify each constituent only to find no buildings
will be left nor will any stones remain upright.

:

From after breakfast to now she's laced the earth
with blood and bone; the same from now until sundown:
this her long weekend. Back-broken from reinterring
the ground slaughter-house waste, she arches her spine,
looks up, lifts a wetted finger to read the future.

:

That so much has gone to spoil in those idle minutes,
that one thing has led to another (a name, a scene,
a phrase, a passerby), that momentary opening
of the private browser, that brief
and unsatisfactory relief, that everything that's sown
in the dark will be reaped in the light.

Naturally, you blame the yellow poison apple, the fruit
of a *whole plant of a ranke and stinking savour.* The earth
with its new layer of topsoil is weed-free and tilled.
A solitary stake marks what's gone and how far there is to go.

Tilt | Shift

For you it's just the brain's last pulse-gasp:
the motherboard emits its final binary twitch before
the circuitry shorts and falls to dark. Sparks of electrons
coalesce to Virgin or Peter, transmit a visitation of angels
to trump them home as they look back on their own
tilt-shift scene of surgeons and machines. Now
Parnia's Shelf sits just below the ceiling, holds two paperbacks
and a picture of the Tower of London. A minuscule,
nearly terminal, lapse in logic, then resuscitation and food.
Tell me, what did you see?

bærlic	hwǣte (white / dazzle)	winberie	ele-bēam	senep-sǣd (synapse / collapse)	fic
barley	wheat	*wineberry*	olive	mustard seed	fig
barely	wait	grape	o live	must seed	fuck
bear me		grave		must-see	
bare me		graven / image			
	weight				
			o lose	miss me	
bury me	way to go		loss		*fin*

Cloud Seed

All dry eyes in the house. Never a mayday piss
on this parade, the Party's apparatus sees to that: clouds
engineered for heavy weather with shovelfuls
of cement (grey), with silver iodide (yellowish) or dry ice
(spectral) by a man stoking a rectangle
of Eastern Bloc countryside through a hatch
at the back of a plane, by a man wiping concrete sweat
from his brow, by a man spitting snow.

:

Would you have forgiven them if they knew
what they were doing? That they were aware the germ
had been growing inside from the very start,
that they deliberately hadn't taken measures?

:

Who are these totalitarian Cnuts
that even the rain and clouds obey them?

Magnetic Declination

Before you go north to her you hem your coat with a row
of bells and tie a length of rope around your left ankle
and dither whether to unroll or roll your jeans. Hat on
or off? You're similarly undecided about covering—or
not—your *Dirty Dozen* t-shirt. Sutherland, Bronson,
Sevalas, Marvin, *and the rest,* emblazoned
across your chest, bursting forth in flame. But, no.
This is no cover-up. It's not the sound of victory, nor
is it the sound of defeat. It's the sound of singing.

:

You watch her finish clearing neglect and shit
of winter from your raised beds. She pauses, unstoops
with hands on hips and the leather loop
from the hand fork hooked over her right index finger.
Taking a marker and the small bag of light-white pebbles
she bought before the fall she writes every seed's name
on a fresh stone and pushes it into the dirt
next to each dibbed hole. Neither Linnaean nor common:
she chooses a new name each spring, each plant.

Notes on the Poems

I. Airworthy

Mary Rose, Henry VIII's flagship, under the command of Admiral George Carew, sank in the Solent on 19 July 1545 whilst engaging French warships. It went down with over 700 hands. Suddenness of the loss of life, and the near-perfect preservation of hull, bones and artefacts in the seabed mud, led Dr David Starkey to refer to the event as "England's Pompeii" (*The Guardian,* 25 January 2008). Lying undiscovered for four centuries, *Mary Rose* was located by archaeologists in the 1960s and raised on 11 October 1982.

viii: "the fair breeze . . . free," is taken from *The Rime of the Ancient Mariner* by Samuel Coleridge, part II.
ix: *Tog Mor* was the crane barge for the *Mary Rose* recovery.
x: the JR is the John Radcliffe Hospital, Oxford, England.
xi: "an iron . . . weft," is taken from *In Parenthesis* by David Jones (Faber and Faber, 2010, p.165).
xii: contains a line drawn from Psalm 127:3.
xiv: contains lines from two letters written by Pliny the Younger to Cornelius Tacitus describing Vesuvius' 79 CE eruption.
xv: the acronym APGAR is used to ascertain the health of new-born babies. Margaret Rule (1928-2015) was the lead archaeologist for the raising of *Mary Rose*.
xix: the Flemish on top of the ship's bell reads 'I was made in the year 1510'—the year that *Mary Rose* was commissioned.

II. Now and Not Yet

'Now and Not Yet': the white horse is a Bronze Age chalk horse carved into the hills near Westbury, Wiltshire, England; the phrase "white heat at the centre of everything" is from Rowan Williams' book *Tokens of Trust* (Canterbury Press, 2007).
'Small Mercies': following the 2011 earthquake and tsunami in Japan, taxi drivers in Ishinomaki reported picking up ghost passengers or phantom fares.
'Matins' contains a line from Ilya Kaminsky's 'Anonymous' (*Deaf Republic*, Faber, 2019).
'Dustsceawung': the Old English word means 'contemplation of dust'; part six opens with lines from Richard Skelton's book-length poem *Beyond the Fell Wall* (Little Toller Books, 2015).
'Five bodies': in 2004 the Los Angeles Police Department released images from its crime-scene photography archives. The titles of the poems are taken from photographs in the LAPD archive. These images, and others, can be viewed at lapd.com, or in the book *Scene of the Crime: Photographs from the LAPD Archive* by Tim Wride (Harry N Adams, 2004).

III. /siːd/

'Insipient' is an archaic word meaning 'lacking in wisdom'. The italicised description of the tomato plant is taken from botanist John Gerard's 1597 book *The Herball, or Generall Historie of Plants*. Parnia's Shelf was an experiment used in a 2008 joint research project between Weill Cornell Medical Centre in New York, USA, and Southampton University, England, to find conclusive evidence for out-of-body near-death experiences during medical procedures.
'Magnetic declination' is the difference between magnetic north and due north.

About the Author

Ben Egerton lives in Wellington, New Zealand, where he teaches in Te Puna Akopai | the Faculty of Education at Te Herenga Waka | Victoria University of Wellington. He holds a PhD in creative writing from the same university, during which he was the Claude McCarthy Fellow. Ben was runner-up for the *Magma International Poetry Prize* (2018) and the *Kathleen Grattan Award* (2019) and shortlisted for the *Beverly International* (2020) and *Christopher Smart/Joan Alice* (2022) prizes.

www.ingramcontent.com/pod-product-compliance
Lightning Source LLC
Chambersburg PA
CBHW030053170426
43197CB00010B/1504